MW00737750

BRILLIANT FALLS

John Terpstra

Brilliant Falls

John Terpstra (signature)

GASPEREAU PRESS LIMITED
PRINTERS & PUBLISHERS
MMXIII

for Mary, and for
my mother, Anna
(1920–2011)

CONTENTS

STORYTELLER

I gave you rocks in a bucket, not flowers
wrapped in paper, not chocolate in a box
and not stones,

which would be too small, you said,
to use as props for your children's story,
but smooth and amiably shaped earth-apples

about the size of my fist.
Perfect, you said. My pleasure, I replied.
I picked them up the street, from the rocky

front yard of someone who wasn't home,
whose cat answered my knock at the door,
emerging from under a bush, curling about my leg,

looking up expectantly at the doorknob, and at me,
and to whom eventually I explained myself,
setting down my plastic bucket, and then,

as though they were the portobello mushrooms
we pick and choose from each week at the market,
plucked rocks, nine all told,

and brought them home to you.
And you said, Perfect.
I did not ask what children's story

requires rocks, not stones, as props,
and I did not look to see if you picked one up
to admire its shape and heft, as I had, nine times—

that buoyant heaviness, which was tinged,
I thought, with a kind of longing.
It was enough that you had asked,

and I could find and gather,
and that after the rocks had served your purpose
I could return them to the yard up the street,

and to the companionship of the rocks
I did not choose for you,
and who, I imagined, as I fit their nine siblings

back into the shapely palms of soil they were lifted from,
may have felt left out, and wondered
what they had missed, what the story was,

looking up at me with their perfect round faces.

WHEELS

After buying a used van on Gladstone Avenue today,
I drove off,
and all the people on the sidewalk
stopped in their tracks, pointed
and began to cheer and wave and throw streamers
from the higher buildings, causing
a big commotion.
All for this used van I bought today on Gladstone,
or so I thought,
until I saw
the Queen of the Commonwealth
in the rearview mirror, tailgating, kissing my exhaust
in a classic '53 pickup, souped-up,
with a hood-scoop,
itching to pass.
She was wearing a halter top
and looked impossibly young,
and I wouldn't have recognized her at all
except for the tiara,
and that distinctive profile, coined
in the side window as she gunned past me,
squealing round the corner like she owned the place,
beating the lights like a local.

HINDSIGHT

The surprise bird, flushed from roadside weeds,
pauses a split-second, weighing its odds
against the firing squad of the front grill,
almost lingers, last cigarette,

then takes the dare, stuns us both
in a sudden dive under the car.
Bad choice. Mirrored in the rearview,
its fleet shape shattered by the metals

that propel us, the bird tumbles a feather-crazed
oh-damn-I-shouldn't-have-done-that
high over the pavement, then swan-songs
the gravel shoulder, a rough black heap.

We travel on in silence, my daughter and I,
our innocence in doubt.

And the plot thickens as later that afternoon,
returning from town, she practice-drives
the quiet concession roads to the cabin,
and I am lulled by her savvy,

her wheel-ease, a natural, the cyclone
of open windows, the music we chose,
when suddenly she swerves,
ploughs into the shoulder's tall grasses.

Dream over. We switch seats.
I back the car onto the road, no big deal,
but we proceed in slow shock.
"I could have killed us both," she cries.

There is the fact of our fragile enormity
upon the landscape, which I forgot,
my young bird, while breezing through
the daring slipstreams of choice

and chancing it—
and the inattentive lapse, yours,
and my own, mirrored
in the crushed grass, and your face.

Because the pain is exquisite and excruciating
when I merely graze my knee against the bird bath,
I bend to sit on a low branch of the apple tree
that graces this garden,
and hear a *thump*,
and turn to see her fallen on the ground.

Because we are so eager and afraid
for all the living things we have no names for,
that will bud and grow and require tending
in this spring of our new dominion,
we have woken early on this first warm weekend morning
to clip and till.

And it's good, working side by side.
We are happy how quickly the beds come clean.
We are doubly happy the raspberry patch,
whose pruning protocol the gardening book
confused for us all winter, revealed its needs
in our presence, its trim canes now poised to bear.

We bend and stand and bend again, and stay too long
in the sun. I graze my knee. She faints.
It's as though a variation on some ancient theme
is being played out. I brush particles of soil
from her face. She rises and goes indoors,
a slight bruise on her cheek.

THE WOMEN OF SHALOM

The impeccably groomed women of Shalom Manor
glide over the corridor linoleum to the dining hall

as though they are walking on water,
by faith, or supported on four-wheel walkers,

their men having already fallen or been made near helpless
by a long life and a less flexible body,

conditions which, by way of contrast,
have imparted to the women a dignity and bearing,

the women who meet our eyes and bestow smiles and nods
as my brother and I move through their midst,

our mother's garment bags, filled with our mother's clothing,
slung over our arms like limp, life-size Heimlich dolls.

As requested by staff, we have been spring-cleaning her closet.
"We'll save one of the dresses," my brother tells me.

I don't understand what he's getting at, distracted as I am
by the upright survivors who traverse this window-tunnel of light

bathed in their own translucence, their smiles
that grow stiff as eyes drop to our burden.

DAD

Picture this. Alone I wrangled your king-size mattress
through the house and onto the roof of the car,

where it lay like the world's largest grilled-cheese sandwich
on a hot day, drooping halfway over the windows,

but with enough life left in it to rear and kick at its tie-downs,
though I drove the back roads processionally slow,

four-way flashers ticking all the way to the dump,
where like some movie alien creature wrestling man-on-cliff

it tried to take me with it over the edge, into the garbage bin,
but fell alone, end over end, to lie upon the rocks, so to speak, below,

where the tides will come and the tides will go,
looking like what it was, an old dead mattress,

the same old matrimonial half-acre as kids we ragged you folks about
for how vast it was, asking *why*, and *how do you find each other,*

appalled at the very thought of your intimacy—and where, alone,
she found you, on the night that all the fight left you.

So, your old Sunday School teacher had it right all along
about Peter at the pearly gates.
"Surname?" the saint asks,

gazing up at you over the rim of his reading glasses
as one by one
he begins to turn the pages of a large book.

"Ah, yes," he says, inclines his head
and scrolls a long finger down the written text.
In the brief eternity that follows

you can't help but notice that the paper
is hand-crafted, possibly Japanese,
and wonder if this is a good sign.

The old apostle looks up at last, removes his glasses and sighs.
He explains that he has no choice.
He seems genuinely sorry

but inadequate funding and staff cuts have hampered research,
leaving your record contradictory and incomplete.
It isn't the first time.

The Keeper of the Keys then confides
that some days he feels no better than a border guard
for a country without enough self-respect to lock its doors,

like Canada. Your heart swells and lifts a little,
a balloon you're suddenly anxious to hang on to
forever and ever.

With a resigned but hopeful, "Anything to declare?"
the saint waves you through,
but not before you've caught the unmistakable, jubilant sound

of a trio
in dire need of a saxophone player,
and you've played the sax, you want to tell him,

almost since the day you were born,
although you must confess
you didn't know that little fact until this very moment.

We are walking in the mild mid-winter
snow and thin ice, up Coldwater Creek,
its many tributaries, their steep ravines
tracing the blue and brown lines that wind
dizzily over the unfolded whiteness of our new
map, like staves for the crazy earth song we've been
sight-reading with our feet. We are singing the impossible
pitch of these slopes and cliffs, losing our place
in a landscape that lives to improvise, and the map
helps, but nothing written is in stone,
and it's always a revelation, stopping to
compare what's on paper with being there.

Because I did not for a moment doubt in childhood
the story of this rising, shall I, now
I am wiser? The world still has no
boundary. The lines still shiver and wave;
the impossible takes place; people are kind.
And these woods are still as real and magic
as when I first chased and followed any path
that found me, and just as fearful, and brown death
still haunts the green, discolouring all
in brilliant falls ground to sodden mulch,
from which, in deepest regions of the wood,
the bright stem still rises, witnessed by
those few who run like children home to tell us.

I'll say this: whom she supposed to be
the gardener sings and dances the contour lines
that are his body; this body that is broken
by time and season and violence too deep
for us to wonder at the source, broken
into beauty that lures our present rambling
and leads us to the edge of this escarpment,
where the waters fall, where all our many streams
cascade and plunge, in curtain and ribbon, over
terrace and washboard
                         (our terms for the living text:
earth's open veins)
                    and where we meet her,
who has run and sung and danced these trails
since the day she first saw
the massive rock dislodged
from the cliff-face
                    of any reasonable expectation.
And all these years removed from childhood
we still leap aboard, to feel if it shifts
or moves us, trusting and not trusting,
not willing and willing
                         the rock to roll on.

THE HIGHWAY THAT BECAME A FOOTPATH

—after the other side won the civic election

And I saw a new heaven and a new earth,
for the first heaven and the first earth had passed away,
and I saw the holy city, coming down out of heaven,
and the holy raving protester who climbed into a tree
to resist the building of the last highway
was still in among the leaves,
but the tree had grown much taller,
and the protester had been living up there for such a long time,
not alone, that several generations of protesters now populated the canopy,
freely trafficking the branches of their swaying neighbourhoods,
as the six-lane highway
wound between the trunks below
as wide only as a footpath,
a red-dirt earthway busy with pedestrians.
And the highway-that-became-a-footpath
led past the longhouse raised
during the same resistance, down in the valley,
for it still existed (both longhouse *and* valley existed still)
and other longhouses,
which were standing at that location several centuries earlier,
had re-materialized, their hearth-fires
burning still; an entire village, thriving
beside the hallowed creek that ran through the east end of the city.
And I saw the trees that formed the longhouse walls
take root, and continue to grow,
forty-thousand times forty-thousand,
their canopy providing all the roof
that the people needed.

And from a privileged perch at the top of the escarpment,
watching as the new city came down out of heaven,
it was clear that the leaves of those trees
were for the healing of the community.

THE SPIRIT OF SITTING BULL RETURNS
TO CANADA, APPEARING AS A HAWK ON
HIGHWAY 13 IN SOUTHERN SASKATCHEWAN

With a deft tail-end twist the deer,
at the last possible moment,
neatly sidesteps the front-bumper's tackle
and lives,
        unlike the grasshopper
who emerges from a dashboard vent,
poses, then pops like corn against the windshield
until I do him in with a tissue.

                    But these two
visitations from the natural order
do nothing
        to prepare me for the hawk
who stands just inside my side
of the broken yellow medicine line
of the highway, stunning and squat
in its buffalo robe of feathers,
its head already turned toward me,
its eyes already wise
             to the fact
that I will need to swerve
          now
as I top another rise
           of rolling shortgrass prairie

to avoid its bloody demise.

Able to, and not much more
than a century or so
late, I do—
                my foot never grazing
the brake.

DESIRE, OR 」

I shot a man las
but only in a d'

He was runn
trying to kee

He promised I coula ık
or even catch up to him

then disappeared from sight.
When he re-appeared in the distance

a stooped shadow moving through
the black trees and the rock

I was lying on my stomach in the snow
aiming a rifle at a spot a few feet in front of him.

I was so surprised he fell
that I didn't fire again

when he stood and stumbled on
favouring the shoulder I must have hit.

PURGATION

Dear God in heaven-on-earth
                             (this river
these friends)
            Why so much shit?

With the others it's once a day, once
every other, that they split from the group,
the site where we're camped (tents up
fire going), and each in turn heads for the woods,
glaring white doughnut roll of tissue
paper in hand as they move through leaves,
tracing a path to the thunder box.

Except for the bugs it's a fine place to sit,
though however much within the forest
you think you feel, the forest can't
pretend that you're not there; and you,
pants-around-the-ankles, propped
on a wooden box, can't pretend
to be blending in.

                  You take it with you
when you go
              downriver, in canoe.
Food, clothing, shelter, a chosen few
items and effects: cleansed
but for the basics, you take it all.
Surprising, in the end (as straps cinch tight

the pack) how little space
it all takes up.

                  Breakfast. Break camp.
Last act before pushing off:
                            toothpaste spat
into firepit, where flames
of campers to follow
                    will kill the scent, and other
whiffs of us (coffee grounds, plate scrapings)
also tossed in
           to keep the animals indifferent.

I enter the forest again. Jack-on-box.
Dear God in heaven why so much of this
stinking to high heaven am I
who I
am?

In the sorry sad state you find yourself in,
        you repeat yourself, incorrigibly.
Ah, well. The world repeats itself.
There is a choice of sounds to select from as you wait:
        a cricket, the Doppler effect of cars passing by
        and low voices through the trees.
Come, let us thrash this one out, again:
        though your sins and shortcomings are numberless
        and expand as the universe is said to expand,
there is love.

Crack another beer.

The voices grow louder.
The neighbours and guests next door in deck chairs overlooking the lake
        punctuate their conversation with bursts of laughter,
        which echo.
The single cricket still contends against the quiet in between.
Meanwhile, out here, far from the city, stars
        overwhelm the absolute blackness of the sky
        yet leave the atmosphere intact with dark,
and as you look up, a visiting dog lays its head upon your lap,
        and with its eyes and body language asks you to understand
        and believe, once and for all,
        that it is always and only about love, unconditional.

Of the cars that have been passing by one finally slows,
    swallows its Doppler, and ascends the drive.
Take heart. Buck up.
These are the ones you've been waiting for.
These are your friends, those tireless smugglers,
    who have ferried their contraband
    love
    across the border and into your heartland,
who swing their car doors open and are reaching to embrace,
having forgiven, already long ago,
your incorrigible self.

Three young women of equal and unparalleled beauty
are seated at the table of a patio café.
Within the past three years,
one of these women has ended
a pregnancy, another
has given birth to a child, a girl,
whom she placed into the open, waiting
arms of an adoptive couple,
while the third is raising on her own
a young son, a toddler.

From a position of complete invisibility
three tables away, you are to choose today
which of these three is your daughter.

The women are young and beautiful enough to stop traffic,
which is exactly what they hope to do.
But they are seated at the outdoor café
only in part to discover if their beauty still holds.
The other part seeks to drown out all voices,
whether hailing a taxi, walking past
on the sidewalk, or taking their order,
in which one of them hears murmuring
the word *murderer*, the other
is repeatedly told she is *no mother,*
no mother, and the third cannot avoid
the wail that rises like a siren
from the throat of her two-year-old,
piercing her rage.

[30]

It is all about these three today, and their bodies,
their lives that are revolving on an axis
that is the single leg of their table,
a flat horizontal surface
that supports their leanings-forward,
their keys, cups, the outbursts of laughter,
like open arms.

There is an urgency here.

From a position of complete invisibility three tables away
you are to decide this day
which of these daughters of heaven
is your daughter,
your sister,

whose life means everything
and all the world.

I am standing before the firing squad of my own mind
for a crime involving a loaf of bread, which is to say
for no crime at all, for the crime of *being,*
when a man in a white coat, wearing around his neck

the stethoscope he soon plans to use on me,
reaches into his breast pocket and extracts a familiar package.
"No thanks," I say brightly, "I've quit.
Those things will kill you, you know."

Given the circumstances I could, of course, relent and have one.
Anybody would understand.
But being not exactly the soul of moderation,
I have learned the hard way that one leads inevitably to another

and another, et cetera, *ad infinitum,* and since a promise is a promise
even to yourself, and since despite appearances
you never really know how the story will end,
why take the chance?

I'd prefer to focus on that loaf of bread,
and on the jug of wine that goes with it (or cider, in my case)—
on her and I, in other words, and on the timeless properties of love
that she's always known so much better than me anyway.

I'd rather marvel at how impossibly far I seem to have come
(knock on wood) from those days when the conviction
I could not live another minute without a cigarette
was like a gun to my head: a gun I discovered only goes *click.*

PRICKED

I have fallen in love with yet another woman.
Is she beautiful? I do not know. I cannot be objective.
She is not a Shih Tzu or a pug,
if that's what you're asking.

The longer she spoke the stronger the attraction grew.
She pointed out adverse reactions
some people have (very few, it turns out),
and I wondered what were the odds

that I was one of those few, or that such a woman
would fall in love with me.
I was conscious of my age, to tell the truth.
She was not too young. Would she be immune?

She touched my arm lightly
just above the elbow, and laughed.
What we were talking about,
I forgot.

Funny, isn't it? I am willing to fall in love
with almost any woman that I meet,
(some more willingly than others)
as readily as others catch cold or the flu.

The woman who works as a labourer
at a construction site up the street.
The last time I drove past,
she was loading bricks into a wheelbarrow.

Even the women sitting in a quiet row
under the dark windows, waiting their turn
for inoculation, and old enough to be my mother—
a scary thought.

The woman I fell in love with last night
had been easing apprehensions all evening.
When she reached to prick a needle into the arm
she had so recently touched, I felt nothing.

A DIGGER OF GRAVES

A pickaxe to penetrate the frost-line in winter,
stones the size of small children:
I do not wish to be a digger of graves,
but am happy to know
not one, but two, who perform this task
I thought no longer exists
unmediated by machine.

One is tall, the other not so tall.
I would like to watch them with their shovels
build a pyramidal range of soil
as they slowly sink themselves down
the four-cornered shaft they are delving
into our body-brown earth.

I am curious to discover,
do they use a carpenter's retractable measuring tape
to determine when they have plumbed,
with their digging,
the required minimum fifty-two inches,

or do they eyeball the depth:
the taller one a point just below,
the not-so-tall to a point just above
his beating heart?

I would also like to be there the next day,
when the family and friends of the departed
have departed,
and only one of the diggers returns to the job-site,
accompanied by his wife and their two boys,

young boys, who hide and seek among the headstones
as he and she together reunite
the pyramid of earth
with the hole it recently was one with—

the loose earth, easily dug and pitched,
their children racing back and forth,
testing the edge, raining
plastic shovelfuls down, their children
wailing
          with glee
at the hollow sound
of a thousand knocks upon the door
no one ever answers.

WHEN I DIED

When I died, fourteen people stood around
and sang a song I didn't recognize
as I was lowered down.

When I died traffic stopped,
and I was carried through the streets.

When I died, no one got around
to fixing the downspout,
and the problems with the foundation
got worse.

When I died everyone agreed.

When I died, I remembered
that one of my lifelong favourite things
was sleep.

UNCLE BERT

You would have enjoyed the scene:
your niece, her husband and two of your nephews,
walking across a parking lot, the men dressed
in black, suit-jackets buttoned, sunglasses,
looking to all the highway, rest-stopping world
like mobsters on a coffee run; your niece, their moll.

Later, the men took the part of honour guard.
Your niece-moll sat in the front row of the church
with Aunt Mary, and sang,
as did we all, a few familiar dirges,
and listened to the usual words. Normally,
you would have sat in the very last row
(so we learned) and been first to leave,
held back from gaining the light of the exit doors
ahead of the hand-shaking preacher
only by Mary's tug on your jacket.
As it was, you were right up front
the whole time, no escape.
She, tugging on a handkerchief.

I want to ask the obvious question:
Was it really you
we escorted out the church
and helped into the limousine?
And how would I know?
                          In the grief
and dereliction of family relations
we rarely saw one another.

Unfamiliar cousins shared sandwiches and cake
at a light reception lunch.
And hesitated to make promises.

The uncle I recall was one of sly humour,
tuned to incongruity and given to needling.
He would have enjoyed these scenes,
as I knew while it happened that he'd have enjoyed
the earlier scene in the highway parking lot,

where, returning to the car, takeout cups in hand,
your travelling mafiosi were hit
by a shot of sunlight deflected
off a windshield; a glint
much like the glint
                        was in your eye
six months back, on the day your niece, my sister, broke
the long spell of absence, entered
your apartment and you said, by way
of greeting, *I remember you.*
                        A glint
that flashed again from the brass
of your highly polished box,
as we let go
                lifting you down to darkness.

AUNT LUCY

Sweet Aunt Lucy, whom I recall most vividly
from Christmases at home, when she sat
at the corner of our living room couch, smoking
the cigarettes she smoked only then,
sipping with a teaspoon from a tiny glass
the liquor-laced egg-nog called *advokaat*;
a nurse, not yet married, with a look of mischief
in her eyes that made me, an adolescent, love her.

Her white hair then and her white hair now.
Her posture as she sits in the corner
of her couch. The summer dress. She and I cover
some of the lost-touch ground that lies between
when those visits ended: her late marriage, the time we last
saw each other, fifteen years ago, and this brief
vacation stop at her apartment. But we do not broach
her brother's, my father's, death.

They were not each other's family favourite.
I remember learning with a kind of shock
how little love ran between the two,
although a kind of love, known as duty,
ensured that once or twice a year he and my mother
would visit Lucy and our new Uncle John, a filial *oblige*
the other couple rarely would reciprocate,
even to missing dad's funeral.

Am I disloyal now in calling on my aunt?
If only she didn't have the same way of sitting,
that same look, which I discover I love still,
in which mischief mostly has been muscled aside
by a widow's necessary might.
My teenage daughter sits across the small room,
innocent of sibling history, and tells me later
that in her great aunt's face she saw
the grandfather she misses.

GEESE

Geese fly low over the roofs of the village.
Big birds. They seem more like the aircraft
of an earlier world
                    (prehistoric, parental,
the looping *m*'s we drew in school
on a paper sky)
                    moving
with more deliberate lack of haste
than you'd think the atmosphere
could support.

The geese converse amongst themselves
as they pass by in small tour groups
above the elderly walkers,
and in their distinct syllables
you can hear the slight correction
of flight path, grammar, instinctual
animal noise, and/or a bland
and absolute ignorance
of where they are.

                    They clear the squat
peaks of retirement bungalows,
swing down, and begin a pond approach,
each bird
            for itself now,
in the near-frantic beating-back of wings
to effect drag, as someone at a cliff edge
might beat their arms in the air

to keep from losing balance.
                              The birds land
feet first and float, wings
smug against the body, as though flight
were only ever
mind over matter.

                    Until I stood outside
on my mother's patio, in this
gated haven, I'd never heard the sky
so physical, laboured, the measured push
against the air, those beating strokes
of manufactured wind as geese rowed
immediately overhead,
                              that feathered breath
against the glass of all this
gravity.

MOM, LIKE THE BUDDHA

Mom, like the Buddha, sits
in her light living room

happy
to go wherever, *whenever*

you have time,
uncomplaining of the hours

spent in her chair, although
it gets boring, she says.

Never cranky; more recently, five years
after Dad's death, shows real joy.

Still, the hours. They weigh.
She sits, not

Buddha, but novice,
having entered

this vow of silence—
a silence not complete

but great.

TULIPS

Driving up to visit in the overcast
weather, I imagine walking soon
with you, getting caught in a downburst
and running (no longer possible for you)
to shelter, laughing.

                There is strangeness
in this windscreen vision, an unsettling
slip of time, like the drop of rain
that trails upward on the glass,
for in it mother and son
are both young.

                What we share instead,
this early spring morning,
is a leisurely paced loop
around the village pond,
your slight breathlessness
near the top of the gentle rising road,

and a pointing-out, by you,
of the clustered spearheads of tulips in the garden,
as we stand sinking with each step
in the grass, soft
from the gone winter,
an earlier rain.

ELDER SON

Something's being hammered home.

The banging telegraphs through the neighbourhood
and dies, briefly, before another rapid-fire flurry,
unconcerned with message, insists
against the atmosphere.

It's not at all like the drips
in the elbow turns of the downspout,
the nerve-wracking, flat erratic tings
making their tortuous way
through tunnels of skin-thin aluminum:

the sounds of a loosening up

that I will not compare
to the indoor hacking of the clock,
which is false in any regard
since its time runs on battery
and should, to my mind, hum.

It's all been said before.
But here's something that's never been said:
I love you, Mom.

Early this a.m.
the patient spiking rat-tat of metal on ice:
someone trying to break winter to pieces.

BONES MEM KNIT

This is the weather of my bones,
and two human sizes in the past
a sweater Mem knit that still fits.

Boot weather. Thick socks.
The pleasant steam of skin under wool.
Tramping alongside the brook

the pebbles tick-tick
and I hear those lightning sticks.
But it will not rain in weather like this.

Above the lap of earth
clouds suspend an endless ceiling
of room without walls:

my old room,
and a heaven on earth
that wouldn't lift, or roar.

In observance of the sixth anniversary of your passing, Dad,
I sank into what has become an annual deep blue funk;
a prison of hating the world and everyone in it, equally,
including myself. For three days, quite literally, hell. For all.
I knew it would last three days from past experience,
and from a suspicion that on some level I'd given myself up,
hoping to reduce the sentence; that you, perhaps, had encouraged this.
Which is how it all worked out, more or less. Handy, to be freed
on what happens to be the day before the doll-on-straw turns real.
And I have you to thank. Assuming, that is, that it is your death
on the straw of your own mattress
that turns the key that starts the engine that drives
these blear excursions through the barred regions of the psyche.
Early on the journey a line flashed past, billboard on the highway,
repeating every few miles. It read ... *and then you die,*
and a few people come to the funeral. Merry Christmas,
Dad, from the little town you left behind.

What happened? Seventy-five years of good health, two of ill,
and you're gone? The place should have been packed,
but it was Christmas Eve, people were busy or away,
and it's not as though the place was empty, but that I
expected more, and didn't know I expected more
until the building didn't fill to the rafters,
and the sky didn't open to angels. Singing.
All those years, the meetings, committees, boards, the willing duty,
what you did with your time when you weren't working.

Mom sits home, doing now what she also did then: waits
for you. You appear, in the form of me: mama's boy, the son
who never left town. She and I take a walk or a drive,
and in the car she is your wife, she is a young girl,
she is my mother, pleased to be engaged in an activity
she so often did with you, and is recognizing passing landscapes
she's never travelled before, and never fails to remark,
You could get Dad to go anywhere.
He'd go anywhere you wanted, but only if he could get there by car.

We go to Egypt, she and I. They have pyramids in that country
to prove it was worth all the effort. Where we never visit
is your cemetery plot, the bronze plaque lying flat in the grass
under the aural realm of a highway,
to stand in the slaughtered innocence of the air above
the neighbouring plaque you also purchased,
with her name already on it, waiting for a final date.

This season's stories have become a mixed message for me,
because your death came so near to that birth.
Your preparations—discharging yourself from the hospital,
having her drive you to the bank—
read as foreknowledge now,
a following of your own dimming star. Each year
I recognize less of what passes by, which once
was familiar as town, tree, child. This time through
I finally thought to ask, *What is it*
between you and that kid?
                              and for a moment I saw you

back in the driver's seat, a three-year-old on your lap,
him, I'm guessing, his hands on the wheel,
the look on your face one I've never seen before,
a wild joy, flight.
                    In this angle of vision
from the passenger seat, it seems easy
to love the world again, forgive all.
Perhaps I could go with that.

EMPTYING THE HOUSE

A man I've never met before
has counted out three hundred and fifty bucks
on my mother's kitchen table
and carried most of her furniture,
including the kitchen table,
and with my help,
out the front door and onto the bed
of his black pickup truck,
letting in a lot more cold air than necessary.

Our mother did not see her four children
for two days re-unite
to clear out, clean, box and save, divvy
give away or dispose of
every single item in her life
not already gone
to furnish the one small
but comfortable room
in the home she recently was moved to.

The furniture looked
much more shabby and used without her
to mend our vision.
It made the work easier,

but we had no idea how much work
she was doing, sitting
in her chair, filling crossword puzzles
by the score, holding together not only herself
but all the smaller stuff
that was so precious to our growing up,

though their potency disrobed,
surprisingly, before our eyes, when plucked
from their familiar groupings
on shelves and furniture tops
and herded onto the table,
where we chose.

You could have spun the table
like the crazy aluminum Lazy Susan serving tray
that none of us wanted
for how the silver teaspoons and stainless egg cups,
the copper, brass, pewter, glass and Delftware
whirled out of orbit
without the gravity of her
at the centre, a gravity they'd enjoyed
with no moth or rust
since forever.

We ventured in
to corners of closets and dresser drawers
private as prayer, places we dared
and desired to explore
only as children,

and grew involved and talkative,
till it got late, too late
to spend, as planned, the small windfall of cash
on dinner together,
and we called for pizza
with everything on it
to be delivered to the door
she would not be opening or closing any more,
and sat on the carpet with paper serviettes—

the beautiful embroidered napkins
placemats and tablecloths
of our mother's hand-crafting prime
having been claimed by my sister
on the first morning we four were together
for the first time in our lives
since forever,
and carefully folded away.

BIRDS

Old birds sit in wheelchairs, asleep
after breakfast, heads
tipped back, mouths open
like young birds.

She is not there yet,

but my mother is immigrating again,
just as she did when she was a young bird
with two fledglings (my older sisters),
and a mate-for-life who flew
their new-world nest of fifty years
not too many years ago.
She misses still his company,
his guiding by the stars.

And this is not the same post-war troopship
she uses for the voyage,
but a boat not much larger than she.
It hesitates, moves in and out,
for she no more desires travel now
than she did at that time.
The restlessness was largely our father's.
One minute she is the young woman
tending fire, making games
on the shoreline of our childhood.
The next long minute
her craft comes untethered, floats free,
and she drifts from recognition.

There is no horizon for her out there.
Water and sky have melded.
The few islands of clarity
tricks of the atmosphere.

I find these days when she is yet in sight
painful.
We are the following birds
who will pause on her craft,
and she will look upon us
as harbingers of a country
she is unaware she is returning to,
although her stories these days,
and even her language,
have reached that landfall already.

Who is my mother?
As if on migration,
we children of a thousand nests
instinctively
fly north, south, home,
are blown off-course and land,
exhausted, on these drifting craft.
We are grateful for life, but afraid
of the timelessness of our parents' ocean,
their heads tipped back as though to receive.

And not one of us knows what to sing.

WHERE HAVE ALL THE FLOWERS GONE?

The girl with the watering can
is standing in a small sea of grass,
leaning over an island of evergreen
that is edged with flowers,
between the four lanes of Route 7
and a corporate spaceship filling-station,
wearing a loose-fitting ankle-length black
nightgown-like dress.
She tips the last drips, gives
the can a shake, turns
in her own world and with a dance step
crosses the green-bladed sea and station pavement,
and enters the ship through a side door

on one of the last mornings of our summer vacation
road trip, thereby animating the view
from the second-storey motel room window—
an unusually well-kept yet inexpensive motel
owned by a refugee couple from Tibet, in whose dream
we have now had a bit part.

There are places you never go
and they are nowhere
and people live there.

Our Tibetan proprietress directs us
to Denny's for breakfast, a restaurant
whose mother ship, like the station's, also orbits the earth.
We know that they're all up there, making us believe

that they make all this possible, and that we owe them
at least the occasional obeisance,
and thus this once we bow, you and I,
and bid adieu to the Dalai Lama, who smiles on us
in the lobby, and give Denny a go,

and he disappoints,
as we knew he must,
although breakfast is not rocket science,
and though the young waitress is cheerful,
and maintains the pretence of meaningful light exchange
as she refills our water glasses, and though the three
men in the next booth are regulars,
and lend these proceedings
the sheen
             of normality, humanity, something
is off or missing, alien even,

and it may be us:
we come from a land so much like this one
it could be a knock-off, you'd never guess …

and I know the girl with the watering can
is leading somewhere as I leave a tip, pay the tab,
and we return, talking in the car, to yesterday's trip
up Mt. Washington, elevation six-
thousand-two-hundred-eighty-eight feet.
There are places we never go, you and I, namely
these tourist sites, as Lizzie Bourne

ought never to have gone
hiking up, in long skirts, likely, starting
so late in the afternoon—
but we broke our pattern, and lived, and found
they aren't kidding about the mountain's wind
or temperature extremes, for within minutes
at the summit she came in sight of but couldn't see
in the fallen dark, your body temperature
was dropping so quickly I saw the light
that left her eyes
leaving yours.

Lizzie was eager to watch the sunrise
from the first tourist hotel in the country, recently opened.
One hundred years later Pete Seeger wrote a song
about flowers, under circumstances that have nothing to do
with climbing above the treeline or the cairn
memorial to her that stands beside the cog railway and is visible
from the window of the gift shop we hustled you into,

but the song attached itself to what I've been writing
soon after I started,
and at the risk of getting maudlin I am going to guess
that this has been leading all along
to my late mother, as most roads do
lately, she shows up
many places, my organizing principle, she appears
each time I open the laptop,

the background photo of her at nineteen,
in a knee-length skirt, straddling a bicycle
that leans against a hedge, the year
the war began—

in a country not much like this one at all.

I'd say she ought never to have gone,
but the alien-nowhere she lived
her last years
unlearned me that
emotion.
We watched, you one side the bed, I the other,
the last drips tip,
the flutter of a dance under closed lids,
and saw her slip
through the side door of a silver ship
which took her to a new home, we hope, in the sun.

ACKNOWLEDGEMENTS & NOTES

Some of these poems have been published previously in *Antigonish Review*, *Centrifugal Eye*, *Fiddlehead*, *Grain*, *Hammered Out*, *Image* and *Openings*. ❡ "A Digger of Graves" was published in *poetry strand summer 2008*, David Zieroth, editor. The two diggers are Al Ernest and Marvin Oldejans. ❡ "Storyteller" was selected as Library of Parliament Poem of the Week by John Steffler, during his tenure as national Poet Laureate. ❡ Poems have also appeared in the anthologies *Roadwork*, Frances Ward, editor (Asphalt Tree, 2010); *Regreen: New Canadian Ecological Poetry*, Madhur Anand and Adam Dickinson, editors (Your Scrivener Press, 2009); and *Henry's Creature; Poems and Stories on the Automobile*, Roger Bell and John B. Lee, editors (Black Moss Press, 2000). ❡ "The Highway That Became a Footpath" was included in *The Best Canadian Poetry in English 2009*, Al Moritz, editor. The same poem was published as a broadsheet designed and printed by Will Rueter at Aliquando Press, in Dundas, Ontario. ❡ Geese and the six poems that follow it in this book were published as a chapbook, *Elder Son*, edited by David Zieroth (Alfred Gustav Press, 2009). ❡ "Birds" and "To a Brother" first appeared in the chapbook, *Brendan Luck* (Gaspereau Press, 2005). Thanks to the editors of all these various publications. ❡ Thanks as well to the Ontario Arts Council and its Writer's Reserve Program for financial support, and to the various recommending publishers. Special thanks to Bryan Prince Bookseller, tireless supporter of the community of writers & publishers. Extra special thanks to the friends and members of the Hamilton Poetry Centre and the participants of its workshops—you know who you are.

Gaspereau Press acknowledges the support of the Canada Council for
the Arts, the Department of Canadian Heritage (through the
Canada Book Fund) and the Nova Scotia Department
of Communities, Culture & Heritage.

Typeset in Octavian by Andrew Steeves & printed offset and bound under
the direction of Gary Dunfield at Gaspereau Press, Kentville, Nova Scotia.

1   3   5   7   6   4   2

NATIONAL LIBRARY OF CANADA CATALOGUING IN PUBLICATION

Terpstra, John
Brilliant falls / John Terpstra.

ISBN 978-1-55447-123-2

I. Title.

PS8589.E75B75 2013   C811'.54   C2013-900308-8

GASPEREAU PRESS LIMITED ◖ GARY DUNFIELD
& ANDREW STEEVES ◖ PRINTERS & PUBLISHERS
47 Church Avenue, Kentville, Nova Scotia, B4N 2M7
Literary Outfitters & Cultural Wilderness Guides